THE LONGEST VISIT

THE LONGEST VISIT

A Memoir

Eli Makover

Full Court Press
Englewood Cliffs, New Jersey

First Edition

Copyright © 2020 by Eli Makover

All rights reserved. No part of this book may be reproduced or transmitted in any form or by any means electronic or mechanical, including by photocopying, by recording, or by any information storage and retrieval system, without the express permission of the author, except where permitted by law.

Published in the United States of America
by Full Court Press, 601 Palisade Avenue,
Englewood Cliffs, NJ 07632
fullcourtpress.com

Print ISBN 978-1-946989-75-8
Ebook ISBN 978-1-946989-86-4
Library of Congress Control Number: 2020914644

Editing and book design by Barry Sheinkopf

Cover art: My family in the mid-1950s—from the left, me, my dad, my sister and my mom.

TO MY MOTHER AND MY FATHER

PREFACE

The idea of writing this book was on my mind for a few years until one day I gathered the courage to sit down and do it.

My memories of my father are vivid to this day, considering that we have been separated for sixty-two years. His absence at an early age, when young children are still in their early developmental stages, left a void that I have carried with me ever since. As I raised my own children, they helped me (without their knowledge) to understand what a boy at the age of nine must have felt in the face of a tragedy. The understanding allowed me to forgive that boy for what he had done, or failed to do, in order to survive.

My mother held the family together after my father's death with courage and optimism, and I continued to learn surviving skills from her. I moved away from her at the age of twenty, but my attachment to her never diminished, and I remain grateful for her devotion to my sister and me throughout our adult lives.

Despite early adversity, I have never lost my determination to endure, to hope, and to dream of a bright future wherever destiny should take me.

This is a story of a victory over many obstacles both in this country and in the one where I was born. In writing my story I hope to continue to set an example to my grandchildren, who, in times of adversity, might draw upon the words of encouragement and hope that life is worth fighting for, that we should feel gratitude to Hashem, and that hard work pays off.

Lastly, I thank the novelist and lover of literature, Barry Sheinkopf, for accepting the challenge of editing my story and succeeding in helping me to turn this volume into a work of inspiration.

—E.M.
Valley Village, 2020

TABLE OF CONTENTS

1: Ward 25, 1
2: The Longest Visit, 7
3: Green Eldorado, 11
4: Chicken Crap, 14
5: Driving Away from Mother, 17
6: Settling Down, 19
7: Eldorado Redux, 21
8: Throwing the Book, 23
9: Aborigine, 26
10: Two Worlds, 29
11: Single Father, Three Great Kids, 37
12: Want To Hang Out?, 43
13: Ends and Beginnings, 47
14: A Bigger Onion, 51
15: Tickling the Keys, 55
16: Another Generation Gives Me Hope, 59
17: Between Two Shores, 62
18: Attitude Shift, 67
19: This Mortal Coil, 70
20: Saying Goodbye, 73

I

WARD 25

THE COMMERCIAL JET WAS MAKING its approach in the early hours of the morning, competing with a slow and lazy sunrise over JFK. I could hear the landing gear coming down to meet the cool pavement of late November. Having sat close to the tail, I had to wait for the passengers ahead of me to disembark, which gave me a few moments to feel the heaviness of my decision to leave my home behind.

While the city was in a deep slumber, it was quietly being painted white by snow descending with its softness on rooftops, trees and streets. No one remembered the last time that it had snowed on the city by the Mediterranean as the sea watched in awe, wondering how such a thing was possible. In the wee hours of that rare morning in a small clinic in Ramat Gan, due east of Tel Aviv on January 23, 1950, I was born.

Many years later, neighbors would tell me that my father was dancing in the streets and kissing anyone in sight.

My childhood was a happy one, largely due to my naiveté and imperviousness to the agony of the a new country just being born two years earlier. Food was a bit scarce, but people were full of optimism and excitement for what lay ahead. From day care through kindergarten and first grade, I was engulfed by loving and caring parents, along with my older sister. And like children everywhere, I took my happiness and stability for granted.

Having been raised on one acre, with an orange grove, on which my father's machine shop was located adjacent to the house that his father had built twenty-five years earlier, we moved into a newly built apartment when I was six.

My father was my hero, my mentor, and the Alamo of my life, but like all fortresses that too was destined to fall into the hands of an enemy that no one could defend against. While a few signs started to show the decline in his health, I preferred to ignore them, clinging fiercely to my hope that he would return to be strong again to defend me against the bullies on our block.

He didn't. And I still refused to accept the verdict. One morning, as he was lying in our only bedroom in the apartment, I told him, "I hate you!"

He replied softly, adding to the burden of my guilty conscience. He never expected anything unreasonable from me and accepted me unconditionally, and, though in retrospect I remember that my performance in school was less than satisfactory, I was nevertheless loved.

The night before I told him that I hated him, we were leaning against the balcony railing of our third-floor apartment when I gathered up the courage to ask him, "Dad, are you going to get better? Are you going to be cured?"

"The damage is irreversible," he quietly replied. It was a terminal disease, though he left out the word "terminal," perhaps because he didn't know it himself—the custom back then was not to tell the truth about such things.

Hearing what I didn't want to hear, I felt a knife tearing at my heart. Something inside me died that night with him. Three years later, he was gone.

From that day on, my life turned into a burlesque, with me creating a separate reality in which I didn't allow myself to feel or hear what was true, choosing to shut out what my heart was trying to tell me: *You are losing him.*

I still remember looking forward to our nightly visits at the British military hospital that had been turned over to the State after the British left Israel.

My dad was lying in Ward 25. Years later, I learned it had housed the terminally ill. During those nightly visits, well after visiting hours, my uncle drove my mom, my sister, and me to see him. Since it was a military base, the one-story corrugated buildings were sited well apart from each other to shield them from air attacks, so our walk from the parked car took almost fifteen minutes. My uncle and my mom told jokes on those walks and cheered me up. I also used to hear the American songs through the open windows as we passed the various wards on the way to number 25. One popular song was always playing— "Green Fields," by The Brothers Four—and it put me in a melancholy but optimistic mood.

A little before 6:00 a.m. on a warm, early September day, my mom, having spent countless nights by his bedside in the ward, slipped into the bedroom that my sister and I were sharing and whispered, "Our father may not live."

I took it to mean *Your dad passed during the night* because, in our family, the truth was not spoken, only implied through a maze of lies and deceptions. Hearing her, I felt a huge relief, knowing that his pain had ended, and so had mine and everyone else's in the family.

But my pain had just begun although I couldn't feel it. I was prevented from attending the funeral at the age of twelve. I had to be sheltered at all costs, as it was presumed I couldn't handle the truth.

Instead, I played in the yard with my neighbor's kid, feeling happiness at last—feeling free!

But the death of my father left a wound that wouldn't heal for many years. I felt abandoned by the man I had loved and trusted, and the feelings of insecurity that swept in manifested themselves in my relationships with teenage girls I was dating. There was one in my hometown with light hair and blue eyes that my neighbor introduced me to, and on my first date, sitting on a bench with her in a nearby park, I kept asking, "Do you love me? Please don't leave me!" and I didn't trust her. She was only sixteen and looked confused.

On our second date, when she opened the door to greet me, I noticed that she wasn't wearing any make-up and took it to mean that she had lost interest in me.

Such were my feelings with most girls that I dated then, arising from an almost narcissistic attitude attuned to my profound insecurities, which blocked any feeling of empathy for others. It cost me many years of counseling down the road.

During my high school years without my father, I found it difficult to focus on my studies and only miraculously managed to pass my exams with grades a bit lower than average.

Then, at seventeen and a half, I was drafted into the Israeli Air Force. The military (predictably, in hindsight) failed to make a man out of me. My growth stalled. I was missing a mentor despite my mom's best efforts. I entered the service a kid and, three years later, left a boy/man yearning to continue my flight, not knowing where I was running to but certain about what I was running from: the pain the place reminded me of daily.

In late November, two months after I finished my three-year hitch, I was lying in bed at night in my mom's and her new husband's large, luxurious apartment. Those nights seemed longer than ever, and I could smell autumn at the break of dawn. My suitcases were resting by the door on the cold blue-and-white marble floor, and as the first light of early morning broke, I got into the new gray suit my mother had bought me for the trip. The taxi took me to the only airport outside my city.

2

THE LONGEST VISIT

THAT MORNING MY AIM was to visit the States, not to settle there. Far into the future, I would call it "the longest visit." My destiny was sealed, although I didn't know it, at the age of twenty.

"Sir," I heard a soft woman's voice saying to me, "please proceed to exit." She looked attractive in her blue-and-red uniform, I thought. I got up tired and feeling insecure about the future and started to the front end of the plane but away from my home, my identity, away from the family that I truly loved and that I would miss for many years.

But most of all, I was running away from the pain that wouldn't heal until well into my forties, when I had finally buried my dad.

Having spent nearly four weeks in New York State, I had landed in Los Angeles on Thanksgiving Eve, in spite of everyone's warning that the smog was out of control. It was 1970, and I would soon be turning twenty-one—a good-looking, naïve, and provincial kid whose knowledge of the city came entirely from the movies and who didn't speak the local language.

My uncle, who was married to my father's sister, was waiting for me beside the yellow Dodge Dart that would take us back to the city. I was impressed, thinking that he must have gotten rich to afford an American-made car with a nice dashboard power steering, and automatic transmission. A few months later, I had learned that in Los Angeles you could put down a hundred bucks and get a car—any car.

A year later, I left my aunt and uncle's apartment to live on my own, shortly after I started working at a restaurant on the Sunset Strip. My arrival in Los Angeles coincided with the tail end of the Hippie movement, all my friends were wearing long hair and waiting on tables, and the movie stars kept on coming for the organic salads with the house dressing they loved.

I was the parking attendant who greeted the customers, who tipped generously. Shortly after I started,

I met my first American girlfriend, who lived with her parents. I was already twenty-one; she was sixteen.

Two years later, after finishing Santa Monica City College and breaking up with her, I had moved into the Valley to continue my studies at CSUN. My English was still quite poor; I hired professionals to write up my school assignments.

The Valley had a different vibe, and I quickly adjusted to the new place. The air smelled like the desert in the evenings, especially during the summers, reminding me of my home back in Israel. Surrounded by mountains that changed color in the early evenings, the air in the valley would cool off, ushering in pleasant spring conditions all the way through the end of June.

Throughout my educational years in Los Angeles, I held jobs that supported me. I worked at a famous shoe store in Beverly Hills until the manager, who was Italian, started to like me a bit too much for my taste, though I couldn't understand what it meant at the time.

One evening he asked me to come to his apartment for a drink, and I accepted. Entering the living room, I noticed pictures of a nice-looking guy but none of women anywhere, only good-looking guys on side tables.

A red light went on in my head then, and I politely

but rapidly left the apartment. I was indignant and quit the job the following morning. I mostly worked in restaurants after that, since the flexible hours allowed me to focus on my studies.

3

GREEN ELDORADO

Los Angeles is famous for its love affair with cars, and I've owned a few. I bought the first for $99.00, a Chrysler that lasted for six months.

The second was a 1964 green Cadillac Eldorado convertible, which I wrecked in a few short months, rear-ending a jeep that refused to move when the light changed to green. Later I drove Volkswagen Beetles and rode a motorcycle. There was also a convertible Fiat 850, in which I got into a horrible accident on Topanga Canyon in the early '70s.

When attending school on Hollywood Boulevard in order to be able to extend my visa, I discovered french fries. They were being sold near the building. I also discovered catchup and Thousand Island dressing, never understanding where "Thousand Island" came from, since there were no islands at all in Los Angeles.

The waitresses smiled at me a lot and kept refilling my cups, even when not asked. That was strange too, because in Israel the refills cost as much as the first cup; in L.A., they were free.

I met many girls during my first eight years in L.A., from whom I kept learning the language and the nuances of the culture. Every girl I got close to asked me, "What's your sign?"

I told them I didn't have one, realizing only later that it was Aquarius, and for the life of me I couldn't figure out why it was so important to them—part of the ambience of the place, I suppose. The cops were called "pigs," and parties went on nightly in Laurel Canyon, where everyone was invited to get stoned. I forgot my old identity very fast as I adapted to my new life. . .and that was a problem. In Israel, I had felt the beauty of the holidays and the sanctity of Shabbat, or the holiness of Yom Kippur; in the States, that had disappeared. For many years it didn't bother me, though, since I was willing to sacrifice a hell of a lot to become Americanized and assimilated.

My apartment wasn't far from Hollywood Boulevard, and I was always looking for movie stars so that

I could write back home about it. I had met a few.

Among the things that fascinated me during my first three years in Los Angeles were the radio stations that never stopped. I set the boom box next to my bed at night and fell asleep to the music that continued into the next day and the next, never stopping. In the car, I never turned the radio off either, and I knew the names of most songs and the performers of the early Seventies. In the summer I went to concerts at the Greek and at the Bowl with friends and co-workers. The money I earned at the restaurant on the strip—it wasn't much—was enough to cover my monthly expenses, tuition, dates, and rent. That was before the price of real estate skyrocketed in the mid-Seventies. My first monthly rent in Hollywood was a hundred dollars a month.

4

CHICKEN CRAP

DURING THE LAST YEAR OF MY STUDIES at the junior college, I had applied for a waiting job at a yacht club on the water at Marina Del Rey, not far from Culver City, where I was living at the time. The club had a high-end restaurant that served expensive dishes from steak sandwiches to exotic fish concoctions and thick, juicy New York strip steaks. We also served cocktails that the clientele ordered to go with their meals. We were required to wear a white jacket with four gold buttons in the front and know the menu and the names of the drinks, and that wasn't easy for me at best. My command of the language was still poor, my accent heavy so that, on more than one occasion, when

I asked a customer who had just returned from a long day's sailing in the Pacific if he and his lovely wife would like some orange juice, the dignified husband would say, "No, tonight we don't want coke." And when a customer ordered a cocktail, I was never able to understand the orders, aside from Shirley Temples and mai tais, since I couldn't catch the names but was too embarrassed to ask the well-heeled boat owners to repeat them. So I pointed out the customer from afar to the bartender, who usually saved me knowing what the regulars drank. "Oh, Joe? He drinks. . . ."

One summer evening, as the sun was setting on the Pacific outside the wide French windows of the dining area and the tired and tan-faced clientele started to roll in, one dignified customer with a stern, red-bearded face and black eyeglasses sat down with his wife at one of my tables. When I brought over the menu, he read it briefly but, motioning it away, asked me impatiently, "Young man, what's the special tonight?"

I vaguely remembered what the chef had said earlier, at the start of the shift, and said, "Tonight's special is chicken crap."

The man's face flushed even redder, and his eyes seemed to catch fire, partially from having drunk beer all day long on the boat. Turning momentarily to his wife, as if to ask whether she had heard what he had, he turned on me and barked, "Bring over the manager!"

We had two managers, one short and chubby but friendly, the other a tall Irishman who looked to me to be in his late forties or early fifties, and who also with a red face and bloodshot eyes. I followed the latter to the table, trembling inside, and when we got there he asked, "What seems to be the problem here tonight, Mr. McKinley?"

"Look here—Eli! Tell the manager what you told us about the special," said the customer.

I answered very quietly, "Chicken crap."

The next few moments are erased from my memory; I only remember the manager yanking me back into the kitchen, shouting in my ear, "Chicken *crêpes*, you idiot!"

I undressed and hung up the jacket with the gold buttons for the last time, all the while wondering how I would pay the rent that was due in less than two weeks.

5

DRIVING AWAY FROM MOTHER

During my first few years in Los Angeles, my mother visited me a couple of times, and that was exciting, since I couldn't afford to visit her. She never understood how I so easily navigated the streets of the vast city without getting lost.

My excitement didn't last long. I had become Americanized and not only outgrown the provincial mentality of people back home but had tried hard to forget the pain that I thought I'd left behind, only to discover upon her arrival that it was still alive and kicking. I tried to hide my disappointment from her but could barely enjoy her company. My issues with my mother were deep, remained unresolved for many years, and with every visit, the wounds would open up, but she had no clue so it seemed. When the time came for her to leave, I drove her to the airport still hoping that there a breakthrough would magically come, enable us to have a heart-to-heart conversation, and at last relieve my emotional burden. I needed badly to hear her say, "Please see me to the gate inside the airport," but all she said was, "You can drop me at the curb—I don't want you to have to park the car." But I *wanted* to park the car, and to feel that she needed to spend a few more minutes with me.

It didn't happen. I sat there behind the wheel like a child who is waiting to be hugged and the hug doesn't come: nothing much left to do but crawl back into a shell to protect myself, as I had done so many times before back home. I got out for a perfunctory embrace, and that was that. It was a big letdown, and I remained silent. Quietly, confused, I got into my car and drove away—back to my American life that didn't include her. Many years later a friend pointed out to me that I had been selfish to leave her behind and come to the States by myself. My friend was right. But my mother never tried to stop me. I might have stayed if she had insisted.

6

SETTLING DOWN

I WAS READY TO SETTLE DOWN during my last year at the university in the Valley and was married in 1977. My first daughter, Liana, was born six years later, followed by her brother, Leor Baruch, two years after that and by Tanya, two years after Leor.

In 1982 I had become a sales and use tax auditor for the State of California, stationed in the Valley. I would retire from the civil service twenty-seven years later to coincide with the birth of two grandchildren, Rachel and Shlomo. My first grandchild, Benjamin, was born while I was still working.

Having lost my dad at a very young age, I have striven to give my children the stuff that I missed in my life at a young age—a full-time presence in their daily life—and I have succeeded at that. In fact, that has been my essence—to be an effective, loving parent. My professional career came second, and it remained that way until I had hung up the gloves in 2011 at the age of sixty-one. Today I'm involved in the daily lives of seven grandchildren.

Before 1977, I was a freshman at CSUN and started to meet other Israeli students who had come over to finish their education. A few returned to the country of origin. I had joined in Israeli/Jewish activities feeling righteous about life-and-death issues such as the plight of Soviet Union Jewry, and had participated in on-campus demonstrations. Campus life was exciting to me, not just the studies but the social life it offered, and like most Jewish students I started to return to my Jewish identity by joining Hillel House and Friday night services that ended with a hearty hot meal.

I must confess it was the hot meals that first attracted me to Hillel House—that and the girls.

7

ELDORADO REDUX

SINCE I WAS LIVING NEAR THE CAMPUS, I didn't need to drive, and my car was mostly parked at the curb downstairs. There was no garage in the building where I shared two bedrooms with my friend and roommate. Going to morning classes, I failed to move the car on cleaning days and, in six months, accumulated twenty-five parking tickets that I had no intention of paying any time soon. One day, an amnesty was offered for delinquents such as I, and I struck a deal with the judge to pay half the fines.

That morning on the way to the Van Nuys Court House, I had recalled another incident with the local authorities, the Beverly Hills Police, five and a half years earlier.

I'd just left at the restaurant one night and was heading west on Melrose in my four-hundred-dollar 1964 green Cadillac Eldorado convertible. I felt the cool summer air through my long hair as I was turning left onto Beverly Drive. At that late hour, all the lights were yellow, requiring a slowdown at intersections instead of a full stop.

I was heading south at 11:00 p.m., with my speedometer registering 65 mph in a 25-mph zone. The street was deserted. Suddenly, out of nowhere, I saw flashing red lights, about three blocks away, in my rear view mirror. My instinct was to dodge the bullet and put on more speed in an effort to lose them, as I had seen countless times in the movies. I had just crossed Pico Boulevard when I noticed two unmarked cars with uniformed police behind the wheel racing toward me. I turned left into Alcott and pulled up in front of my girlfriend's house. It was quiet, and the flashing lights painted the street red. Five cars converged on mine, and I gave up.

They cuffed me and hauled me to the station. I had been arrested for unpaid parking tickets. My girlfriend bailed me out, paid the $40.00 outstanding fees, and at 3:00 a.m. I was once again a free man.

8

THROWING THE BOOK

THE UNIVERSITY HAD A NICE LIBRARY where I spent so many hours that it became my second home. I was dating different girls then and was working part time. At the end of the winter semester, we would go on short trips in VW Beetles, drink beer, and dance and sing until 3:00 a.m. I thought that this pleasure would last for ever and continued to feel my self-esteem rising every time I aced an exam—and they were not easy due to the language barrier. The other benefit of being at the university was that, every time a person asked me, "What do you do?" I could proudly declare, "I'm a student."

I had met fathers on some of my dates who were

not too happy with their daughters' choice, and others were glad to have me. Being from Israel naturally opened doors for me, not just into my girls' homes but beyond, as was the case in my auditing career.

On my field journeys to audit the various business, I would meet their representatives—American Jewish accountants located primarily on the Boulevard in the Valley. When I walked into their offices, they immediately asked some personal questions. The first was always, "What's that accent?" (thank God, not *What's your sign*).

And I replied, "What accent?" To me, an accent was French or Chinese.

"Where are you from?"

"I'm from here," I shot back.

At that point, the short and chubby bespectacled accountant would start to feel agitated. "I mean, where are you originally from?"

"Oh! From Israel."

"Ah! I *thought* so, but I wasn't sure. . . . Did you serve in the Army?"

"Sure!"

"Wow! . . . Nancy, please make Mr. Makover some coffee. "

"Thanks, Mr. Goldberg. Shall we start now? . . ."

But Mr. Goldberg remained there in front of me,

still deep in thought, as if trying to picture me with a rifle, shooting at the enemy—not knowing that I had only held a rifle in boot camp and never after that because I wasn't a combat type—too romantic and sentimental to kill a fly, much less an adversary.

"Please," he eventually said, "follow me to the conference room, where the books are, and please don't hesitate to ask Nancy for anything."

I had won him over instantly, and that wasn't uncommon during my career. My Asian co-workers had had a much more difficult time with the accountants, who could be difficult and uncooperative due to mistrust.

But there were also some unpleasant days when I wasn't liked and treated badly, almost abused, such as occurred one morning when the representative had left me in a storage bin where the records were located and turned on the heat. It was the middle of August; I was locked in there for three hours and hated him. I subsequently threw the book at his client in revenge.

9

ABORIGINE

AT THE UNIVERSITY, I WAS TORTURED by anxiety ahead of every exam. I simply couldn't get used to the butterflies in my stomach, the worry that wouldn't leave me. I had learned to live with it, anticipating the great rewards that lay ahead for me—like a woman after her first pregnancy who, despite the hard labor and pain, chooses to have another child, and another.

At 1:00 a.m. on a warm Sunday morning in July 1984, Liana Bracha, my first child, was born at Cedars Sinai. At that hour, the hospital was dead quiet and deserted, the smell of lemon disinfectant rising to my nostrils from its shining yellow linoleum floors. But I could still feel the excitement: The palpable atmosphere of good will in the place was welcoming, since it was where babies made some of us parents for the first time.

I was feeling fatigued and running on adrenaline. I should have been asleep but was about to participate in the delivery of my first child and take real-time pictures.

I saw the crown appearing and disappearing back and forth, like ocean waves near the shore, now receding, now emerging. That had lasted almost forty minutes when, suddenly, the OBGYN nurse stopped the show and asked me to grab my Minolta and shoot pictures for posterity. Cell phones wouldn't be invented for another ten years.

At first I was startled by the request, not realizing that the show *could* stop for a few seconds, but I snapped out of my reverie, took some pictures, and hurried back to my coaching job.

She came out with head full of brown hair, lips as red as cherries—and her face as red as an aboriginal too, her face perfectly round, her brown eyes intelligent.

The nurse, whom I didn't actually trust at that hour of the morning, handed her to me momentarily, and I saw the snowflakes that covered her soft, unadulterated body. The skin felt magical to my touch, covered with vernix—and the experience was so utterly novel to me, so *original*, that I have never forgotten it.

At 2:00 a.m. that morning, my life would never be the same as it had been five minutes earlier. I had become a *dad*. I thought about my own father and how he had literally been dancing in the streets in January 1950 in the snow that so rarely falls there.

I walked out of the room and embraced the first person I saw, a male nurse who didn't seem too surprised. A few days later, I was wondering if he'd taken it the wrong way, because he asked me out. Blushing and feeling queasy, I declined the invitation but thanked him.

Three nights went by at the hospital; the next morning, we placed Liana in a car seat and drove her home. She looked tiny and lonely in that huge car seat.

10

TWO WORLDS

MOVING TO A NEW COUNTRY has a big advantage. You can re-invent yourself and be what you want to be without needing to convince anyone, since no one knows you.

Back home I had to live up to certain expectations that kept me down and made me doubt myself. In fact, when I stopped living up to what I was supposed to be, I finally found myself—though not without hard work. This newly found freedom to re-invent myself and come into my own helped, however, to widen the gap between me and the people I had left behind a few years before. And that included my sister.

On her visits to Los Angeles, I could see the newly emerged difference between us. She remained the way I remembered her—naïve—while I felt that my life had reached new levels that I didn't think she could understand.

For example, I had developed survival skills, since I could no longer rely on anyone to help me financially. I was always a paycheck away from being homeless. I had left the shelter of a family that was usually there a safety net to help me, and been forced to rely on myself. I was alone and insecure in a strange land.

She was not, and a part of me resented her sense of security, which I no longer had and which she couldn't fathom because she'd never left her comfort zone. Seeing the opportunities around me had given me the motivation to work hard and be independent.

It took me many years, well into my thirties, to learn to make decisions and trust them, but once I became aware of my inefficient old behavior that didn't exactly work well in my new home, I was able to change it and grow. These changes can only happen when you leave familiar terrain in life and take risks, like leaving what you know behind and start stumbling forward in alien spaces.

Since my mother was working at a bookstore in Israel, she sent over hundreds of books, and I translated them as I was reading from Hebrew into English. My command of the language had improved immensely, partly because of the nature of my work, in which I was constantly writing reports that described the findings of my audits and taking many communication courses that the state sent me to.

So I was endlessly sensitive to the two worlds—Israeli and American—that I inhabited and that crunched and slid against each other like tectonic plates.

But I lived at one and the same time in two other worlds as well—the one framed by my own childhood, and the other framed by what I discovered in my own kids' childhoods, from which I learned perhaps even more about myself.

I had been anxiously waiting for Liana, as intervening pregnancies had ended in miscarriage, and I was fully ready to get into the parenting role. The experience that I had with Liana was a bit different than what went through my mind and heart as I was watching my boy grow up. Through the different stages of his childhood, I kept having flashbacks to my own life as a boy and reliving my feelings at those times for my own dad. So when Leor was seven, I was able to see myself in him and suddenly it became much clearer to me what must have gone through *my* mind at the age of seven in relation to my own father. This wasn't a small burden for me; it added a measure of sorrow and insecurity to those flash backs.

That went for a few years, triggering more awareness that helped me begin to appreciate how I had survived those years from a perspective of a child. I was able to contact the stages of my own emotional and intellectual intelligence. Consequently, I began to forgive myself for what I had done, or failed to do, growing up in the face of an adversity that left me totally lost for the lack of a way to express what I was going through, since my sense had been that no one would listen. The result had been a life of burlesque, the truth hidden deep inside me.

I had thus unexpectedly gone through a therapeutic experience with my boy that I hadn't with his older sister.

But Liana had the benefit of having her parents all to herself for three years, while her siblings had to share theirs from the beginning. Still, she had adapted to her siblings and treated them fairly, serving as a good model for their development. In that respect, she was also helping me with my parenting: I trusted her judgment.

Leor was born on April 1, 1987, a lovely spring

> 7-21-86
>
> Dear Liana,
>
> Your 2nd birthday celebration was yesterday at "Will Rogers State Park" and it turned out beautifully. Kalk and I have been telling you about all the kids who would come to your party and about the horses at the Park preparing you in advance for things to come. You were bitten by a bee, early in the morning, and handled yourself remarkably as usual. I took you to the ranger's office to ask for an advice. We applied ice to your little finger to numb the pain. People started to arrive at 10:30 and they kept on coming. Although you were supposed to be the center of attraction you preferred keeping a low profile. We went to see the "Polo" game, played ball, frisby and ate peanutbutter & jelly sandwiches. Kalk baked a beautiful and very tasty chocolate cake and made home-made toys for all the kids. Your freinds had a real good time, I can assure you, and they will probably remember your party for a long long time. Happy birthday my dear baby.
>
> K.K.

Letter to Liana, 1986

night— fooling everyone. Like his sister, he made his debut at Cedars, two hours before midnight. The doctor, who was going through personal challenges,

6-17-88

Dear Son

You are 14 months young and adorable. It is easy to take care of you. ~~and~~ Every night I bath you; you climb into the tub by yourself as of last night. You love books; the other day I asked you, in Hebrew, to go into the den and bring me a book to read to you, you went and brought a book, climbed into my lap and stared at the pictures with joyfull interest.

Your eyes and facial expression speak to us so clearly with no need for words. Since you were an infant, you were able to communicate with us successfully.

I can not help but kissing your face all the time; I love holding you in my arms with your chubby cheeck next to mine.

Grandma sent sandals from Israel, they fit you so beautifully, I'll save them for you. Take care little one.

אבא

Letter to Leor, 1988

showed up late, so the nurses delivered him. I had to leave the hospital after he was born and return to Liana, who was being watched for a while by friends in the Valley. So, unlike my experience with Liana, I didn't get to spend the first and second nights of Leor's life with him.

Three years earlier, I remember sitting by the window on the tenth floor. It was 5:00 a.m., and I was holding Liana in my arms, watching the darkness outside disappearing slowly as a new day began. The trees were completely motionless, and the birds were just waking up. Her mother and I had taken shifts holding her, preferring to have her with us in the room at all times.

But I was very quickly bonding with Leor as well.

Tanya was born in the spring, like her brother—on March 10, 1989, at Kaiser Hospital in Woodland Hills. It was a pleasant Friday night, a little earlier. I stayed with her until sunset on Saturday before returning home to take care of her siblings.

She was fair, on the light side, with ocean-blue eyes and silky blond hair. Her first few months were difficult, since she was colicky, and I was in my early forties, with a bit less strength and having a harder time getting up at night to feed her and still wakeup on time to go to the office.

6-29-89

Dear Tani

You are 3½ months young and very beautiful. People tell me you look just like me, I can't tell. But I hope you do.

Your blue eyes are alert and soft at the same time. You are easy going and already have a personality. I love kissing your chubby face and hand.

Liann and Lear love you and you begin to recognize them as being close to you. Neighbors and ~~friends~~ friends love to hold you and you let them with no problem.

I begin to feel closer to you and try very hard to give you ~~overall~~ a equal attention. You are a pretty secured baby and we'll continue to support you in the best way possible

Love you
little one
Abk

Letter to Tanya, 1989

11

SINGLE FATHER, THREE GREAT KIDS

A FEW YEARS LATER, MY MARRIAGE STARTED to fall apart. We separated in 1990, and our divorce was finalized two years later. The divorce process was agonizing at best, and at times I thought that I might lose my children, as their mother tried to move them out of the state. Five whole months and ten thousand dollars later, I had managed to stop the move and continued to be present and involved in their upbringing.

Being a single father was challenging anyway, and I found strengths I never knew I had. I had always thought that it took a village to raise a well-rounded child and allowed the teachers at the school and community leaders to help me. The children had the benefit of a supportive community and seemed to lack very little as a result of the breakup.

Sending three children to private Jewish day schools took a financial toll on me as well, since my salary was pretty low and I was paying child support on top of the school tuition. My co-workers drove new-model cars while I made do with jalopies and, on more than one occasion, blew a tire on the freeway.

We had been crammed into a two-bedroom apartment for many years, but the children hadn't lacked my attention and care. Due to the nature of my work, I had had flexibility to take time off on a moment notice in addition to having health and dental insurance, and the paycheck that always came at the of the month added stability to our family. I certainly struggled more after the divorce.

While the custody arrangement was in their mother's favor, a few years later it was modified, and the three children lived with me at least half of the week; by the time they became teenagers, they were with me almost full time.

AND SO THE YEARS PASSED. I had dated a few women without ever intending to tie the knot again. The children liked a few of them, but none of them spent the night in my apartment when the kids were with me.

The main reason I had decided to stay single, however, was this: During my marriage, their mother and I had had many disagreements about raising them, some involving religious issues. After the divorce, I had the freedom to raise the kids as I deemed best, and I liked that freedom. Although at a loss on more than one occasion, for the most part I felt confident and received some professional advice from time to time from the therapist that I was seeing.

ONE BY ONE, THE CHILDREN CAME into their own in different ways that complemented them as a team.

Liana was the leader of the group well into the teen years. Tanya observed her sister's behavior and took mental notes while respecting her lower position on the totem pole. Many years later, after she got married, she surprised us all as a grown-up woman, wife, and mother. While I always had a sense of her strengths, I didn't grasp them anywhere near enough. Tanya started to show terrific management skills in financial planning. After high school, she enrolled in nursing school, following her sister's career path, and became a top-notch nurse at Children Hospital Los Angeles.

On my walks and hikes with Tanya, I also started to get to know her better as a woman and to trust her more, and on different levels, than I had before. She became a trusted friend to me beside being my child. I hadn't expected that— it was one of many surprises that life throws at all of us. Having kept inside me many hard memories related to the breakup many years earlier, I was suddenly able to share and unburden my mind and my heart. Tanya and I saw eye to eye on many issues, as I discovered later.

Years later, Liana and I went hiking in the Santa Monica Mountains on her days off when the kids were at school. On those morning walks, which lasted a little over an hour, we shared feelings and thoughts that were quite intimate and confided in each other as good friends do. As with her sister, I had long found her a smart, mature woman whom I could trust with my feelings.

That trust went both ways. Liana and I share a few things in common. We love physical workouts and music. And in her early thirties, we even covered a song together in a recording studio. She continues to compose and write music.

AFTER HIGH SCHOOL, LEOR ATTENDED the University of San Diego and left the nest. That move proved seminal, as he stopped living Jewish Orthodox life. While the change came over him rather fast, I wasn't surprised. I remembered how unhappy he had been in Orthodox high school and how he yearned to enroll in a conservative campus in the city.

But the school was too expensive, and I'd had no choice but to keep him in an Orthodox school, where I had received generous scholarships. While Leor felt stifled and restrained, he found ways to cope. He broke every rule in the book and got away with all of it, largely owing to his suavely charismatic, charming personality. Other kids were thrown out of that school for breaking similar rules.

One rule was that no boy could meet a girl anytime and be alone with her. When he turned sixteen, I had bought him an old Mazda, and he headed straight to the richer side of town outside Beverly Hills, where he started meeting teenage girls. He also had a talent for earning money and sold doughnuts at the school at a high profit, which paid for the gas. He got up early in the morning and headed out to Crispy Cream in Van Nuys to buy three dozen doughnuts, and sold them all. Not once did I receive a phone call from an unhappy parent complaining that his kid was consuming too much sugar thanks to my son's capitalistic ventures on the high school campus.

A few years after graduation from the University of San Diego, and later Pepperdine School of Law, Leor passed the bar and started practicing law.

Gallery

My mother, Geula Makover, 1990

My father, Baruch Makover, 1960

My sister and I, 1950s

I and my sister, 1968 (photograph by Avram Chai)

My children, Liana at the top, Leor in the middle, and Tanya on the bottom, 1992

Eli Makover
Senior Tax Auditor

Sales and Use Tax Department
15350 Sherman Way, Suite 250
P.O. Box 7735
Van Nuys, CA 91409-7735

(818) 384-2090
(818) 904-2449
FAX (818) 901-5252
Eli.Makover@boe.ca.gov

Although I carried this card for 27 years, it didn't define who I am. It was a practical decision at best to go into this field, as my passion was elsewhere.

12

WANT TO HANG OUT?

TRAINING NEW AUDITORS WAS part of my routine, and I had trained many. One afternoon in August, I and one of my trainees were assigned to audit a small restaurant in Rowland Heights; it was in an Asian community, and on my break I walked into a market to buy an apple. Upon leaving the market, I was chased by the manager and a security guard, who accused me of stealing the apple and threatening to arrest me.

My trainee's face turned white, and I was startled and froze for a few seconds, processing what I had just heard. I was familiar with the culture since many of my co-workers were Asians. I regained my composure and slowly reached into my back pocket producing a receipt for a single apple: eighty-five cents.

My trainee later told me that he had been ready to throw punches at the two for humiliating me in public. But I'd kept the incident under control, and later suspected that the owner of the restaurant next door, who was under audit, had sought revenge and collaborated with the market manager to get it.

One hot August morning, I hunched over the general ledger in the oval conference room of a high-end car dealership in Calabasas. The room was lavishly decorated although not to my taste. A large crystal chandelier hung above the massive oak table, and there were two sliding doors, one to the right of me and the other on my left.

Suddenly a petite and shy-looking young woman in a red dress entered the room and asked me whether I knew where the break room was located. I said I'd just gotten there. She was an auditor from another agency that had been assigned to work there that day. I got up and, together, we followed the strong aroma that led us to the coffee room.

As she and I sat across from each other sipping the hot brew, I felt an instant chemistry between us. Like me, she was an immigrant from a country in the East and had taken an American name so that people could pronounce it easily.

When we were finished and got up, she asked, "Do you want to hang out sometime?"

Without thinking, I replied, "Yes!" Her directness and unassuming manner arrested me. Her eyes were light brown and intelligent, reflecting a soft soul in the morning light; her hair fell straight onto narrow shoulders, and she wore flat shoes. In the early evening, when I walked her to her car, we exchanged phone numbers and started seeing each other.

With every passing month I became more attached, although I didn't fully understand her way of thinking and traditions, which were foreign to me but nevertheless intriguing.

The first two years together we cooked and ate at her studio apartment, not far from where I lived. Her profession was similar to mine and, unexpectedly, our cultures shared some commonality.

One late afternoon in the second year, we were on the way to Palms Springs for an overnight excursion when an argument broke out in the car. My instinct was to turn the car around and call the whole thing off—but then I heard her say something completely neutral. It instantly calmed me, and I realized that we were not feeling the same thing, not interpreting the situation in the same way. The insecurities and nervousness that I had felt and brought into the argument were apparently unfamiliar to her. She stayed calm, but tears appeared in her luminous eyes, and I was stunned. While my behavior was self-destructive, hers were self-*con*structive: She wanted to keep driving and put the argument behind us. A layer of insecurity, a flimsy fence, peeled off inside me, and our hearts moved closer.

That night, lying in our dark, quiet hotel room, I understood her better, and my selfish attitude resolved into an emphatic feeling of great tenderness toward her. It persists to this day, and will continue, I think, indefinitely.

Ten years later—I'd already been retired for nine— her career took her away from Los Angeles. Our meetings became more infrequent as time went on. But the physical distance that life has thrown at us hasn't diminished my feelings or my sense of caring for my best friend and lover. The story has been written, the words spoken, and my heart has long allowed her to enter me. While the future isn't ours to see, jealous of its secrets, it doesn't matter. I learned a few years ago that love transcends physical barriers because it's already in the heart and soul to keep. And I've also learned that "the love that we keep is the love that we give away," like a bird that cannot be caged, and that, if it stops flying, it will die. Loving a person is allowing her to be what she wants to be, for the minute that you introduce limitations, your happiness will begin to slowly die.

13

ENDS AND BEGINNINGS

STRUCTURE BRINGS SECURITY TO SOME but not others. In time, I started to live with freedom from financial worries, from failed relationships and bad company. I know today, at the age of seventy, that I should be grateful for what I am receiving and not worry about how long it will last, knowing fully well that all things end in time and new opportunities present themselves.

At the end of May 2011, I took the short walk from my office to the exit door of the building and out to the street for the last time, leaving behind twenty-eight years of civil service with the State of California. It was a love–hate relationship, and while

I loved the flexibility, I hated the low pay. I also liked meeting different people from many different nationalities, but having to be the policeman who kept taxpayers honest was stressful. But the many Goldbergs and Icebergs and Rosenbergs on the Boulevard made it tolerable. I was proud to represent the state and was at the top of my class in number of audits settled, always finishing the assignments in a timely fashion.

The past nine years have brought six new grandchildren, and all my children are married with kids. I now have seven grandchildren with whom I am closely involved.

IT HAS BEEN ALMOST HALF A CENTURY since I had landed that winter morning in JFK. During my short stay in New York City, I met a stunningly good-looking woman ten years my senior who lived in a Park Avenue penthouse. We had a brief love affair, and she had followed me to the West Coast for short stays. I was turning twenty-one. Blonde, blue-eyed, and about five-eight, she was the woman of my dreams in a forbidden love affair that could not last long. I could barely speak English, but that didn't matter.

I remember speeding at eighty-five miles an hour with her—there were no cameras then—on the way to Las Vegas in a rented red Chevrolet and, for the first time entering mesmerizing Sin City. Instant terror took hold of me at the sight of the glare and size of the hotels on the strip. Only three months in the States, I was a provincial kid from a small country that only saw such extravagance in movies, from a safe distance.

I wanted to shut myself in the hotel room and never come out. We were standing inside the Grand MGM Casino, in the blinding glare and the thick smoke, when, with tears in my eyes, I suddenly grabbed her ivory-white hand. From a moral point of view my mind couldn't accept the idea that gambling was okay. She didn't understand this, could not fathom my sudden insecurity, not realizing that all of it was totally foreign to me. I wasn't Americanized yet. I was a kid from a small place, with slim experience, who had ended his military service just five months before.

She must have loved my innocence; maybe it reminded her of what she had already lost. She was a model in New York and one of the pioneers who took off her upper clothes for pictures in fashion magazines.

On my first Saturday in Manhattan when she and her wealthy, plastic surgeon husband went for a ride in the family Rolls Royce, I looked around from the back seat through the large, gray-tainted window and asked them in surprise, "Why is everything open and looking like every other day of the week? Don't they close the stores on Saturdays?" they laughed and looked at each other, a bit perplexed but in forgiving attitude, mumbling something that I didn't understand.

14

A BIGGER ONION

IN 1982, WHEN I HAD JUST STARTED to work at the Board of Equalization, I met a co-worker who instantly attracted my attention by his manners and wisdom. He seemed to know quite a bit about the Jewish biblical traditions and—to my amazement— actually quoted the scriptures.

Twenty years later, he would become my supervisor and a close friend with whom I could confide freely. I loved the philosophical discussions that we used to hold at his office during the day to break the routine, and his memory was incredible. A couple of years before I retired, we became the hiring team at the office and, just before retiring, had hired about fifteen new auditors.

That function was pleasurable for me, and we continued to bond. I liked interviewing the young, attractive women straight out of the universities. He and I complemented each other in a mutual effort to find good candidates. I was a sentimental interviewer who could tap into the character of the candidates, and he was the logical and more analytical one. Together we were a winning team, and our hires performed well, fit the organization's mission, and were promoted.

He and I ended our career on the same day in the spring of 2011 and continued our relationship in the years that followed, meeting at the Coffee Bean for a cup of coffee or hot chocolate and a short walk, when we would reminisce about the old days.

There were a few other co-workers that I got close to and kept in touch with after I retired. A few of the young auditors that we hired texted me for years afterward, remembering me and thanking me for the break I had given them to embark on their careers. It felt good to be remembered.

Like an onion with most of the layers peeled off, my core began to reveal itself and I began to re-discover who I am. No more burlesque. Inevitably, we erect fences around us for protection and to adapt to prevailing conditions in order to reduce vulnerability. That is also true when we get into relationships—trying to impress people and wanting their approval, especially at the office, where we seek promotions to earn higher salaries. The same is true for people who own their own business. They must satisfy their customers in order to compete successfully.

This is a cycle we all experience, and the onion gets bigger as we move away from who we really are. The masks are on our faces and on our hearts for many years, until we get old, retire from the economic race and no longer need to satisfy a boss, a customer, whoever.

I felt the burden coming off me when I didn't have to pretend and play a certain role any longer. That change also came to my relations with my adult children. Overnight, like a snake in the fall, I shed off the layers that had kept me away from myself, from my heart, and started to listen to, and engage in, meaningful conversations. I ended the race. I could walk slowly and at my leisure, throwing away the loud alarm clock. I had time now.

But time wasn't exactly on my side, I discovered as I climbed in age. Mondays became Fridays rather quickly. It was okay with me to gain years, but I refused to become an old man.

Twenty years earlier, when my son and I shared a small bedroom during his high-school years, I used to drive him to the gym. That was before he got his driver's license and the car that took him over the hill to meet the cute girls and break school rules.

A couple of years later I was driving myself to the same gym twice a week before going into the office—for a morning workout.

I fell in love with the gym and never stopped exercising to keep my virility for my own benefit and that of the women in my life.

15

TICKLING THE KEYS

ONE HOT SUMMER, DURING THE LONG vacation when I was in the third grade, a big black upright piano was delivered to our third-floor apartment, purchased for my sister as a bat mitzvah present and to encourage her to learn how to play. I remember, in the mid-to-late 1950s, accompanying her and my mother to an Eastern-European immigrant named Mystros who taught her classical piano. I liked to sit and listen to her at home and at recitals until one day, when I had just turned eight, I sat down and started banging on the white keys.

I played a few tunes by ear and got better and better . . . still only on the white keys.

In a few short years, I was playing a variety of pop songs, and neighbors who passed under our balcony would stop and listen to the familiar tunes. People from my neighborhood told me how much they had enjoyed listening to my playing without me knowing it. It warmed my heart to hear that, some sixty-plus years later.

The piano is still standing at my sister's apartment in Tel Aviv, but she stopped playing it in her late teens. I continued to improve and will play the piano to the end of my days.

There have been times when I had stopped—during my studies and marriage, I couldn't afford a piano. But right after the divorce, I rented one and began to play again.

At first I felt I was navigating through uncharted waters, but something interesting soon started to develop. I was growing and expanding my range, venturing to play on the black keys as well, and expanding my skills immensely. The first two years were hard, with many mistakes, but it didn't matter—I had found the courage to take risks and venture into newly discovered methods of playing, enriching the sound in the process beyond my wildest imagination. Recently, at the age of seventy, I learned to play a Chopin tune.

The piano became a therapeutic tool as well that

comforted me profoundly during my years of despair after my marriage broke up. The kids were still little, and I only had them one night a week and every other weekend. But I continued to see them daily, as I was driving Tanya to nursery every morning and preparing the other two for school, since their mother had to leave for her job at 7:00 a.m. But my nights were free. I wasn't dating while enrolled in group therapy for two years following the divorce.

At 4:00 a.m. one morning in January 1994, the earth shook violently, and the piano collapsed. I had returned the original one by then and rented another.

A few years later, I acquired a beautiful black upright that's still standing in my living room. I feel a deep emotional connection to it, and I believe it will continue to serve my grandchildren for many years to come.

Living alone, the nights started to make me feel lonely. And here is the dilemma: Although I am seventy, my spirit is young and I prefer to be with younger people, who make me feel fresh and strong. Many women I dated after my divorce wanted to get married. I didn't. My marriage was not a good experience in its final three years, and the divorce was very painful. I gave up on marriage after that and have seen no need for it since.

In time I stopped seeing my friend on regular basis;

I was still unavailable emotionally. I remember going out on a date a couple of years ago and sitting in the living room with a lovely woman next to me. She suddenly turned and said, "Please kiss me."

I was surprised and unsure of myself. I've never considered myself a good kisser, but I complied—and felt very little sensation. My heart was closed, and I didn't even know it.

The next day I confided to her that I had no intention of committing, and she left me. I didn't resent her. I simply realized the new reality I was in, and to this day am still hoping to meet someone to travel with and share new experiences.

16

ANOTHER GENERATION GIVES ME HOPE

As I write these lines, we have been hit with a pandemic never seen before, requiring months of quarantine and isolation. The economy came to a standstill. No vaccine has yet been found, and millions of people have been infected all over the globe. I miss my family and hope the restrictions will be lifted soon, allowing us freedom to hug and kiss again. And my grandchildren give me hope for a future beyond this terrible viral scourge.

Less than a year ago, my seventh grandchild was born at Kaiser Hospital in the City. Leor and his lovely wife became first-time parents. I'm elated and beside myself as I see the child developing weekly and changing between my visits. He was born prematurely but was strong from the start.

I remember visiting him at the Hospital in Woodland Hills, where he was staying for three weeks after he was born. I watched his courageous, intelligent parents enduring the initial surprise and painful weeks to come.

Tanya helped with professional advice, reassuring us of the baby's health and progress. Every day was suspenseful but full of hope. I was impressed with both Leor and Maxine's resilience and cool nature under stressful conditions. Every time I asked them about their son's condition, I received a cheerful report full of hope. He finally was discharged and came home in good health, to every one's relief.

MY SECOND YOUNGEST GRANDCHILD was born in the Spring at UCLA Hospital in Westwood. As I was walking toward the hospital from the parking lot, I remembered how, forty-seven years earlier, I used to wait on tables a block away at a popular restaurant on the Boulevard. On Friday nights, a couple of musicians played, keeping the customers happy, and the tips were good. I was twenty-four, and the cost of living was low, allowing me to afford a one-bedroom apartment in Culver City and a small car. I ate my meals at the restaurant, cutting down the cost of food. That was before I finished Santa Monica City College and transferred to CSUN.

Reaching the front desk, I asked to see Tanya Makover and was shown to her room, where I met him three hours after he was born. I loved him instantly and bonded quickly. This was late on Friday afternoon, and I had to get home before the Sabbath started.

MY THIRD YOUNGEST GRANDCHILD was born at Kaiser Hospital like her brother before her. It took me a bit longer to bond with her, but a couple of years later we became very close and bonded. I love watching her dance and carry on conversations with her.

17

BETWEEN TWO SHORES

FOR MANY YEARS AFTER REACHING these shores, I refused to become an American citizen: My sense of loyalty to my home country ran deep. One may make the argument that liking peanut butter and apple pies automatically qualified me, a hard argument to resist. But in my mind, I was always at home away from home, feeling lost between east and west of the Atlantic. That notion, of somehow not entirely belonging to my host country, remained with me for a very long time.

And the unfinished business I had in Israel magnified that sensitivity and kept tormenting me whenever I went back to visit.

As the airplane touched the runway at Ben Gurion

Airfield, I started to feel inexplicably sick to my stomach and at first thought it was motion sickness. Passing the passport-checkpoint stations on the way to collecting my luggage from a humming carousel, the heaviness of the moment released an avalanche of emotions that completely overwhelmed me. Ambivalence crept into my heart, vying with excitement and nostalgia.

I started feeling insecure and uncomfortable on my way to the exit, where in a moment or two I'd meet my mother and sister, who were waiting to drive me back to the city where I was born and raised, my "real" home, only to find that, there too, I no longer *belonged*. Everything, and everybody around me, looked and sounded familiar but felt eerily strange. And I was reminded of a novel I had read a few years back in an English Lit class at Santa Monica City College—Jerzy Kosinski's *The Painted Bird*.

In it, locals in a remote village in Eastern Poland would capture a bird, paint it with bright colors, and release it back to the pack, where it was rejected and viciously torn apart by the other birds.

I had become painted, I realized with a shock, and no longer belonged there; I had become different, a foreigner, an alien. And while my mother and sister looked cheerful and happy to see me, I felt a stranger among them too, and ashamed for feeling so. A low-grade nausea soon set in that lasted the entire visit.

I felt weak and bewildered, imagining that the two of them were exchanging furtive glances, thinking, *My, how he's changed. He's speaking Hebrew with a slight accent—can you hear it? His posture, even his manners, are American now, and he's no longer one of us.*

Yes! I became a strange bird indeed.

The discomfort intensified with visits I later made on with my young children, and on one occasion I was actually admitted to the hospital for a few hours with stomach pains. But there was nothing wrong with my *stomach*.

The source of the discomfort that these visits aroused in me was rooted in memories that were evoked when I saw my family and the places where I had been raised.

And the sense of unfinished business I felt so unerringly, and so at variance with what I yearned to feel—ease, joy, *home* —was this: I had left that home less than two months after my military service ended. A year before, my mother and my sister had married. In my sister's case, I'd had to vacate the one- bedroom apartment that we shared (my mother no longer lived with us when she remarried) and move in with my grandparents and, later, to a rented room with a nearby family. I felt displaced without being capable of articulating that displacement. I was still a kid (veteran of the Israeli army or not) and had no foothold on self-awareness.

My sister married a lyricist and children's-book writer from a renowned family in Israel. We were close in age and both narcissists who competed vehemently for her attention. I watch in agony how tormented she became trying to satisfy us both.

As it turned out, he wasn't her soulmate, and her marriage ended in divorce a few years later.

My mother had married a man ten years her senior whom I had nothing in common with, and once again emotional strife set in, with my mother in the middle of it. He passed away twelve years later.

Since I had felt all along that I'd contributed significantly to the emotional mess surrounding us following both of those marriages, I decided to leave, to run again—and this time far enough away to ease the pain that had become so familiar, only to discover later that I had packed it in my own suitcase that November morning when the taxi driver took me to the only airport outside Ramat Gan, Ben Gurion.

And that in a nutshell (though nothing is quite that simple) was the unfinished business it took me so many years to resolve.

The early-Seventies song by Neil Diamond about being lost between two shores describes me pretty well. Growing up in Israel, one develops a strong sense of nationalism that culminates with serving the country in the military—a rite of passage for all men and women alike, albeit with a few exceptions among the Ultra-Orthodox yeshiva boys whom religious leaders discourage from getting drafted. That Zionist zeal that I was brought up on restrained me too from wanting to become a United States citizen. Many of my friends cherished the idea and became naturalized. I hemmed and hawed about it for the next twenty-one years.

18

ATTITUDE SHIFT

IN MAY OF 1991, I BECAME A U.S. CITIZEN and swore to uphold the U.S. Constitution and bear arms in defense of the nation. But I still didn't feel it in my heart, only on paper.

I returned to the office after the seminal ceremony with a small American flag in my hand, one of which had been distributed to the two-thousand-plus men and women gathered that morning in a hangar in downtown Los Angeles, some with tears in their eyes fulfilling a life dream and ending a life of oppression—such as refugees from Vietnam, Iran, and other totalitarian societies.

During many encounters and discussions with co-workers and friends who had emigrated from these countries, I found that they felt great relief in having successfully escaped in their quest for a better life for themselves and their offspring. That hadn't been the case with me, because I hadn't run away from a *country*, but for personal reasons involving my family. I had simply exchanged one democracy for a much bigger one fifty-one states.

It's true that Israel, like Great Britain, has a parliamentary system, but it's still a democracy with a president (even if that president serves only as a symbolic figure).

About twenty years after I became an American citizen, my attitude started to shift. Los Angeles at last had begun to feel like home, and I had ceased to feel disloyal to the place where I grew up as I admitted to myself that I had become an American in mind and heart. My children and my grandchildren had all been born here too, adding to my sense of belonging and ending the internal conflict. In recent visits to Israel, I have no longer felt the discomfort and ill feelings triggered by meeting the family. I have reconciled the difference and grown to love both countries.

Today, from the purchase of advanced age, I feel, at the risk of sounding naïve, that I finally understand the meaning of what my life has been. After all my name isn't Victor Frankel (*Man's Search for Meaning*). Looking back, and can acknowledge that I made some good life choices that produced desirable outcomes that also laid the ground for my children, who've followed in my footsteps and excelled well beyond my own achievements.

I have few regrets. As the kids were growing up, I asked them to meet local marriage prospects, so that they wouldn't move to the East Coast. I have lived a fuller life due in no small measure to their living near me.

Now, with luck, I'll live another twenty years in good health—a criterion that children can never comprehend, since I have already lived two thirds of my time here and they're still on their first. This is especially true, of course, of my grandchildren; as I play with them, I can't help but realize that there is a strong chance that they will not have me in their lives somewhere in their twenties. That has been a factor in my urge to write this narrative. I owe it to them so that they will have a point of reference and a greater sense of familiarity with Saba.

I wish I'd had an opportunity to get to know, better than I do, the feelings and thoughts that animated my own grandparents' lives. Although I have vivid memories, they were not intimate enough.

19

THIS MORTAL COIL

THIS LEADS ME TO AN ISSUE that most people in their seventies begin to think about. I've been pondering the acquisition of a gravesite, which I suppose is a natural enough progression in most peoples' lives. Like them, I'd like to minimize the burden of death on my kids and make a clean exit.

In conversations with my peers and grown-up children, the issue has come up from time to time. My daughter Tanya has already told me she won't come to visit my grave because she carries me in her heart. Okay, I can die with that. Both Liana and Leor say they *will* visit me, and I'm glad to hear that, too.

At 4:00 a.m. on a Saturday morning, the phone next

to my bed rang, and my cousin broke the news that my mother had just passed away in a Tel Aviv hospital.

When you move away at a young age from your parents, you inevitably run the risk of not being there when they need you the most as they become older and more frail. Luckily, my sister had never left Israel and *was* there to help our mother in her hours of need, especially during the short hospitalization prior to her death. I had known about her condition, but no one revealed the seriousness of her illness to me, or I would have flown back to sit at the bed side.

Sounds familiar. . . .

On Shabbat morning, upon entering the Chabad of North Hollywood where I had davened for many years, I asked the rabbi if I should leave at the end of Shabbat. I was hoping to attend the funeral. "Yes, of *course*," he said.

A few hours later I was on an Air France flight back home to bury my mother.

To my surprise, I didn't experience heavy grief that day and remained focusing instead on staying strong during the entire week of mourning.

But shortly after I returned to LAX, that grief began in earnest. My heart started to hurt, and my blood pressure rose to levels I had never seen. I started to feel a low-grade nausea that lasted almost a year, and my doctor put me on an anti-anxiety medication. Still needing to go to the office every morning and into the field to audit, I relied on those pills to hold me together and give me temporary relief. Tanya took me to the emergency room one night when my level of anxiety spun out of control. But I continued to function and take care of my children, who were living with me full time.

Looking back, I remain astonished that her death hit me that hard since, she and I had lived very far apart by then for almost twenty-two years, and I honestly believed that I was no longer attached to her.

I was dead wrong.

20

SAYING GOODBYE

On my visits to Israel, I visit my father first and then my mother, since they are buried in different graveyards.

As I walk from the car to my dad's headstone, I can smell the pine trees lining the narrow path that leads to him. I have to be careful not to trip and step on other graves.

Most of the stones are broken and cracked, but my father's is holding up pretty well. My heart pounds in my chest like a hammer, and I feel great sadness coupled with the awkward, jagged feelings of unfinished business. I didn't get to genuinely know him. I was twelve when we separated.

I touch the cold stone; I kiss the cold white marble and talk to him, knowing full well that he's watching from above, since his *neshama,* his soul, departed long ago.

He left so quickly after that brief early-summer evening conversation we had on the balcony, while leaning against the metal rail. I will never know why *Hashem* took him so soon, and the only explanation I can find is this: *Hashem* took a father from his young son but would bring that son three angels to father and raise. So one child lost a father, but three children gained one.

Throughout my early years of parenting, I kept asking God to spare my children the pain I had gone through so early in my life, and I was granted that wish. Thank God, today they are in their thirties, and I still give them pep talks and do my best to instill wisdom and life experience in their minds.

Then my sister and I drive to visit my mother, who is in a newer cemetery outside Tel Aviv. The drive takes twenty-five minutes.

I am captured by different emotions when I touch the cold stone above her; it's a mixed bag, due largely to having known her for so much longer than I did my dad, and having gone through many heartaches as well as happy years with her. I know in my heart that she always loved me unconditionally, but I would be lying if I were to write that my relationship with her was flawless. Far from it. I didn't get a chance to interact with my father beyond my childhood, so he has always remained perfect in my eyes and heart.

Statistically, American men live on average to eighty-three—with exceptions, of course. On more than one occasion I have told Tanya that I have a contract with God that he can take me in my sleep at eighty but, until then, to please grant me a full-quality, illness-free life. Tanya doesn't like that and has asked me to renegotiate the deal to extend the time to age ninety. The older I get, the easier it becomes to agree with her.

It feels good to be where I am. I don't have to be right; I'm okay and you're okay (a terrific book in the late Seventies) is my attitude today. I'm reminded of a story that I once heard: Students of a great rabbi gather around him to hear something important about life. Time passes. Finally he says to them softly, in a voice trembling with great wisdom, "Life is a river."

They contemplate this for a while, until one of them says, "But, Rabbi, what do you mean, life is a river? How could it be so?"

"Okay," he replies with a smile, "life isn't a river."

And now that all my children have children of their own, I can rest assured that they can understand, and feel, the love that parents feel toward their children. And so I say to them: "Do you know how much you love your children? Now you know how much I love you." I suspect that people who don't have children (out of choice or otherwise) don't live a full life, and can't get the full meaning of what life is about.

I AM REMINDED, AS I OFTEN AM, of Frank Sinatra, my favorite performer. I too have lived a life that I call full, and traveled on plenty of highways.

God bless.

www.ingramcontent.com/pod-product-compliance
Lightning Source LLC
Chambersburg PA
CBHW020105240426
43661CB00002B/40